716

To: Gabe!
Happy Birthday!

With Love,
Grandma + Grandpa

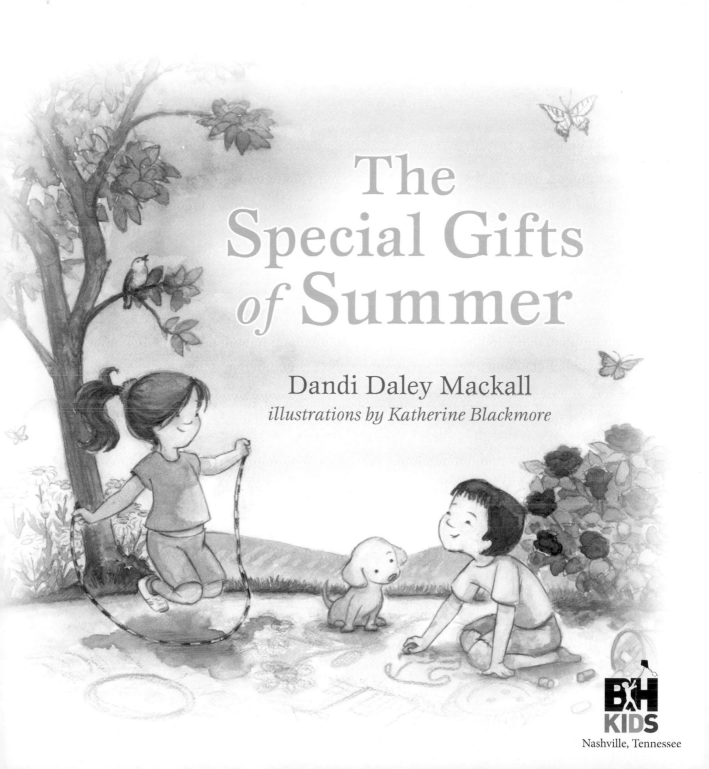

The Special Gifts of Summer

Dandi Daley Mackall

illustrations by Katherine Blackmore

B&H KIDS

Nashville, Tennessee

Dewey Decimal Classification: J508.2
Subject Heading: SUMMER \ SEASONS \
INDEPENDENCE DAY

ISBN: 978-1-4336-8235-3
Printed in China
1 2 3 4 5 6 7 8 - 19 18 17 16 15

He changes the times and seasons; He removes kings and establishes kings.
He gives wisdom to the wise and knowledge to those who have understanding.
—Daniel 2:21

God created everything—
Summer, autumn, winter, spring.
See what summer blessings bring. . . .
Thank You, God, for summer!

Jesus shines His light on me!
Days grow long, and I can see
Summer gifts—they're all for free!
Thank You, God, for summer.

May his name endure forever; as long as the sun shines, may his fame
increase. May all nations be blessed by him and call him blessed.
—PSALM 72:17

Summer hollers, "Come outside!"
Time to take a wagon ride—
Mom and Dad are by my side.
Thank You, God, for summer.

The one who lives with integrity is righteous;
his children who come after him will be happy.
—PROVERBS 20:7

Fill the pool right to the brim.
Dive on in and have a swim,
Splashing 'til the sun grows dim.
Thank You, God, for summer.

Praise Him, sun and moon; praise Him, all you shining stars.
—Psalm 148:3

Plant a seed. It's time to sow.
Soon the corn will start to show.
Only God can make it grow.
Thank You, God, for summer.

"For just as rain and snow fall from heaven and do not return there without saturating the earth and making it germinate and sprout, and providing seed to sow and food to eat, so My word that comes from My mouth will not return to Me empty."
—Isaiah 55:10–11

Thanks for lemons—lemonade?
Stretch on out in summer shade.
Time to watch our town parade!
Thank You, God, for summer.

And there will be a booth for shade from heat by
day, and a refuge and shelter from storm and rain.
—Isaiah 4:6

Happy birthday, U.S.A.!
Freedom! Independence Day.
Watch a fireworks display.
Thank You, God, for summer.

Now the Lord is the Spirit, and where the
Spirit of the Lord is, there is freedom.
—2 CORINTHIANS 3:17

Run through sprinklers! Chase your friends.
Race or tag? It all depends.
Summer fun that never ends.
Thank You, God, for summer.

Our mouths were filled with laughter then,
and our tongues with shouts of joy.
—Psalm 126:2

Summer fishing when it's hot—
Some are biting. Some are not.
That's okay! I love this spot.
Thank You, God, for summer.

"Follow Me," He told them, "and I will make you fish for people!"
—MATTHEW 4:19

Feel that sunshine on my cheek?
Let's hunt treasures by the creek.
Fossils! Rocks! Just take a peek.
Thank You, God, for summer.

He cuts out channels in the rocks,
and his eyes spot every treasure.
—Job 28:10

We could take a mountain hike,
T-ball, baseball, ride my bike.
What in summer's not to like?
Thank You, God, for summer.

From the rising of the sun to its setting,
let the name of Yahweh be praised.
—PSALM 113:3

Let's go camping! Grab your tent—
Hot dogs to my heart's content,
Sweetbriar, campfire, heaven-scent.
Thank You, God, for summer.

The smoke of the incense, with the prayers of the saints,
went up in the presence of God from the angel's hand.
—REVELATION 8:4

Summer shower—*pitter-pat*—
Soaked clear through in nothing flat.
Thank You, God. We needed that!
Thank You, God, for summer.

"I will send down showers in their season—
showers of blessing."
—Ezekiel 34:26

Chilly breeze this afternoon,
Fading to a crescent moon.
Smells like fall will be here soon.
Thank You, God, for summer.

Harvest has passed, summer has ended.
—Jeremiah 8:20

Remember:

May his name endure forever; as long as
the sun shines, may his fame increase.
—Psalm 72:17

Read:

Summer is a time for enjoying the sunny world God made! And whether you're at the beach, the lake, a pool, or just running through the sprinkler, a lot of your summer fun involves water. The Bible tells us that Jesus offers a more important kind of water. In John 4:13–14, Jesus says, "Whoever drinks from the water that I will give him will never get thirsty again—ever! In fact, the water I will give him will become a well of water springing up within him for eternal life." So although that cold glass of water feels great on a hot summer day, Jesus' living water offers something even better—eternal life with Him!

Think:

1. Why do you think God chose to make four different seasons? Why not just one? Or five?
2. If you could do one special thing all summer, what would it be?
3. Think about summer memories with your family. Which one is your favorite?
4. List three of God's blessings that you can only enjoy in the summertime.
5. Summer vacation usually means that families have extra time together. Can you think of a way your family can use that time to do something special for Jesus?

Do:

Make an ocean in a bottle.

1. Fill a small water bottle about halfway with water.
2. Add a few drops of blue food coloring to the water and then add enough cooking oil to fill the bottle most of the way.
3. Add small shells, glitter, or a bit of sand.
4. Glue the lid back on to the bottle. Close tightly and allow to dry well.
5. Rock the bottle side to side to create ocean waves and remind you of all the wonderful summer blessings God has made.

When you feel the warm summer sun, thank God for His love!